SEHNSUCHT

SEHNSUCHT

CHRISTINE MCNEILL

All rights reserved. No part of this work covered by the copyright herein may be reproduced or used in any means—graphic, electronic, or mechanical, including copying, recording, taping, or information storage and retrieval systems—without written permission of the publisher.

Printed by imprintdigital
Upton Pyne, Exeter
www.digital.imprint.co.uk

Typesetting and cover design by narrator
www.narrator.me.uk
info@narrator.me.uk
033 022 300 39

Published by Shoestring Press
19 Devonshire Avenue, Beeston, Nottingham, NG9 1BS
(0115) 925 1827
www.shoestringpress.co.uk

First published 2020
© Copyright: Christine McNeill
© Cover image: Christine McNeill

The moral right of the author has been asserted.

ISBN 978-1-912524-63-1

ACKNOWLEDGEMENTS

Acknowledgements are due to *Agenda*, *Oxford Poetry* and *The Frogmore Papers* in which some of the poems, or versions of them, first appeared.

"It all begins with *Sehnsucht*…"
– Nelly Sachs (1891–1970)

CONTENTS

Outing	1
Light entering by the back door	2
Looking	3
November	4
Owl watch	5
Kings of the air	6
Lark	7
In a Japanese garden	8
Solitary	9
Summer afternoon	10
Ways of feeding	11
The life of a letter	12
Third element	13
Gustav Mahler at *Attersee*	14
Missing	15
Absence	16
What you have missed	17
Shooting stars	18
Vase without flowers	19
Soul leaving	20
A mark on the rug	21
Dog waiting in *Paradise*	23
Seen	24
The kite	25
Crossing	26
A walk on the dark side	27
Sun and candlelight	28
Blue foal, a child's picture, 1912	29
Question and answer	30
In his employment	31
Winter	32
Bringing down a tree	33
Ways of seeing	34
Pink flamingos in the English countryside	35
The real me	36
One day	37

Steam in the kitchen	38
A suitcase for my mother tongue	40
Birth of a philodendron leaf	41
The Beethoven cat	42
The Panther's escape	43
We can reach the magic wood	45
The connoisseur	46
Hair	47
Crossword	48
Grey cushion	49
The offer	50
Bazella wa riz	51
Home	52
Epiphany	53

OUTING

Your car moved away like a whale
freed from a sandbank,
out into the open
I did not know.

We drove through the countryside,
stopped to pick berries,
scrambled around the ruins of a castle,
picnicked in deep woods.

Time unmoving in your face
we passed what your steering hands held.
Wrapped in a dream of myself
I drew the final minutes of the return journey

in long, winding threads.
You parked at mother's home:
my heart slid out of the door—
ignition running like a tender muscle—

and I too small to say what I felt.

LIGHT ENTERING BY THE BACK DOOR

Unexpected guest,
wary to come further. Child
from outdoors, unsure
to enter barefoot.

I watch it light up the carpet,
soften the apples on the windowsill.
It smiles behind a corner.
Feel free, I want to say.

It is shy.
Afraid, may vanish altogether.
And reappear somewhere else
in stronger disguise.

LOOKING

At times I just want to
watch the rain
against the dark yew-hedge.
Watch for as long as it lasts,

then marvel at the sun
breaking through the clouds
to make me see fat drops like jewels
on the washing line.

And here in the kitchen
a batik painting whose colours
are running free
in my eyes.

Such moments.
Look, I say, and hear myself answer: *Yes.*

NOVEMBER

Gloom at 2 pm.
Rain, not knowing
where else to go.
A dormouse darts ahead
like a gloved hand.

From beyond the hedge
the fluting of a robin

takes me far out
into a greater dark
that says
I'm getting to know you.

OWL WATCH

In a wood at the foot of a Canadian mountain
we stare with binoculars into the dark of a tree
where a Screech Owl might nest.

We pour out tea from a flask. Hours pass.
Tonight this wood is our home.
I keep awake by pondering what *home* means.

The dark makes it seem as if we'd been born into it.
We imbue it with hope for a living spirit
until our vigil becomes mere longing.

A small child, one night I ran from the dark
through a glass door, breaking it with my arm.
The wound grew into something bigger than me

until the consternation of others diminished it.
I was held, the blood staunched,
shards removed.

Daylight ghosts over the tree-tops
and we're still waiting;
by evening we'll be back in our garden

with its scent of lavender and lemon-balm,
and from the porch a radio voice
will pour like warm milk.

KINGS OF THE AIR

They arrive overnight in early May,
arrow round buildings,
taking food on the wing,
parting the sky,
letting every summer
drop down at once.

Their flight flows into the city streets
where the sun widens its pool of light
to a redstart perched on a twig
of yellow-blossoming mahonia

and the old man picking bus tickets
from a litter bin
walks on
into a morning of validated journeys.

LARK

Listen to the lark
pull up its bag of trills
from the ground

to rise up,
letting it drop
over the long field.

Walk with me
as high in the sky
it follows my steps,

and in our moving
we're part of what the air gives
and takes away.

IN A JAPANESE GARDEN

I wish I could see again that moment
a heron statuesque all afternoon by a pond
with a flick of its head caught a koi,
gulped it down
and lifted off,
circling the garden in a farewell
to the small group beneath with walking sticks,
rollators and wheelchairs;

circling again this oasis of spring

and again, as if drawing a halo
over this silent company of heads

then flying away over the urban roofs.

No one had noticed.
But an old man
watching a small boy running
round and round the blossoming cherry tree

muttered under his breath:
I wish I could still do that.

SOLITARY

It is one of those mornings
when he comes to join me
on the bench by the lake.

Each time I get up to leave
he holds me back
with another story

as if his old age
cannot let go of my youth.

I look out at the water
where two swans
regard one another

while he chooses words
solitude has given him.

The sky's broken clouds
mirror in the water—
Above as below, he says.

An overhead branch
sends its reflection of leaves
into the still lake.

The swans draw closer.
That's how it was for sixty years, he says—
together.

The swans drift apart.

One bird
blazing white
protects what lies below the surface.

SUMMER AFTERNOON

Washed and hung in neat pleats
the white net curtains played with
the sun in a breeze.

Into my semi-conscious dozing
came the shrill call of birds,
followed by wedding bells.

I went to the window:
the walnut tree shimmered in pollen and light;
the birds had found shadier places.

But a hawk, plucking a caught dove,
looked at me, asserting its right
to be there in full sun;

white feathers in a timeless drift—
and I couldn't change anything,
only watch.

WAYS OF FEEDING

His carer feeds him shredded iceberg lettuce
while chatting about bee-eaters and orioles.
The surf of a blue sea comes to him
as he swallows hard. Orioles
with golden wings
along a coast
carrying a treasured secret
to another land as the spoon
leaves his mouth.

He trusts her moves. Now she talks about
a Laughing Gull, with twitchers on a village green
to catch a glimpse.
He's never heard of such a bird.
It would be good, he thinks,
to take leave of the world with a Laughing Gull
as company.

Have you ever seen one?
A new supply of green makes its way to him.
No, he mutters.
A Laughing Gull, come all the way from America.
Like him, it won't stay long.
Water, he whispers.
Waves come to him
in the shape of a spoon with dangling bits
and a Laughing Gull—
deep below where he is
everything is blue.

THE LIFE OF A LETTER

An envelope pushed through the door.
Unfolding the hand-written sheet,
surprise on her face,
a secret
hushed by a finger on lips.

The writer's voice
released like a genie,
she sees him tall
as if a seedling had instantly
become a tree.

His adventures glowed on the page.
Happiness in life, she read,
depends on the nature
of one's thoughts.

She pondered on this
until the furniture drew close
as if to see for itself;
and she began losing the sense
of his scrawl—

their being friends
that had meant for so long
one soul in two bodies.

THIRD ELEMENT

This space between
the pen in my hand
and the blank page
is like the silence
amid our spoken words,
a ghost
of something unsaid
edging in,
a third presence

that gives no inkling,
and we carry on in the same way.
Only after one of us
has left the room,
it makes itself known:
that life-giving *Ah!*
surprised *Oh!*
that thoughtful *But* …

and space breathlessly fills
and flows.

GUSTAV MAHLER AT *ATTERSEE*

Shaded by the linden tree
he watched the steady
progression of clouds
that seemed to him to be moving
from one life
into another,
and he with them.

Not the patches of clear sky by the mountain,
nor the birds singing (which he had ordered to be killed),
but the clouds
inspired the first chords of his Third Symphony.

He walked with them in his thoughts,
each note cradled by the wind.
The chirping, warbling, trilling birds
lay lifeless on the ground.

But *he* couldn't be driven from this place:
the lake
now meant nothing.

Only the overcast sky made him feel
cloud and soul lay side by side.

MISSING

She cycled out into the sun
away from dark feelings
into the road that was like
a giant green leaf.

She cycled along blossoming trees
away from fear,
light in the saddle,
escaping the words *I can't cope*.

She pedalled away from being grown up
into her small child's self,
stopped for a picnic,
listened to the birds

who listened to her
and came for crumbs.
No, she wasn't on drugs,
only gave herself

to the silence
between natural sounds.
They reported her missing.
She *was*: had missed the child in herself for too long.

When she reappeared
she drew on the misted up window—
the way we sometimes have to
on what is opaque.

ABSENCE

It is as if the chair you sat in
were beating like a heart.

A book open on the table,
a sharpened pencil half on the desk,
half over the edge, in space.

That time you sat before a pot of tulips
bearing tight-lipped buds:
I want to see the flowers open.

I see you sitting after it had happened:
the petals showed their hearts to the sun.
Or did you not witness the exact moment?

The pencil balances on the edge—
weightless in the shadowy dark.

WHAT YOU HAVE MISSED

The chronic pain in the lower back,
incontinence pads, forgetting names,
skin bruising at the slightest bump.
The daily question about bowel movement;
the not-caring-anymore if you do it in bed;
the feeling after waking
of being in a balloon swaying from side
to side, taking off, not knowing
where the damn thing would land.

Someone explaining for the umpteenth time
that the wrist-alarm works by pressing the red button—
knowing somewhere in your mind that the sea is
too far for you to ever see it again;
the path through the vineyard too haphazard—
a voice saying old age is no fun.

But you've also missed the sun on your face
turning life into kindness, and you
inwardly moving as if on thermals, smiling
at the dead in your bones.

You've missed feeling thankful for a painless day;
a spoonful of ice-cream a blessing on the lawn;
a bird's song having more meaning
than a symphony in a concert hall.

One should leave this world at eighty, you said,
fell asleep and never again woke.
Sleep, gratuitous gift from the gods.

SHOOTING STARS

We pitched the tent on the lawn.
You read how long ago shooting stars
were called the tears of St. Lawrence.

Martyred on the night of the tenth of August,
at the moment of his death
they fell, like rain.

Snug in our sleeping bags we listened.
Listened to the fire within us
joining the cool air.

A comet's grains of dust begin to glow
when entering the earth's atmosphere—
that's what shooting stars are.

When the hour came,
we watched—
and wished;

hoping our wishes would last
through the next seasons,
or to the grave.

VASE WITHOUT FLOWERS

It's stood there for ages, but today
I saw it as if for the first time.
No special light, just my eyes straying to
that corner and settling
on the gilt vine leaves on white porcelain,
Japanese, so graceful
even without flowers.

You carried it home in a shopping-bag.
No one on the bus suspected
the contents weren't groceries.
Climbed three floors to your flat.

Would never have thought that by
placing the vase just there
years later I would have this moment

of smelling lime blossom:
you would never have dreamed
an empty vase
could do that.

SOUL LEAVING

I wonder if it's like this: a miniature *me*
stepping out of my body.
Perhaps not *stepping*, but gliding away
on cushions of air;
no more breathing, no looking back;
pushed forward as if on a swing,
dropping all thinking and feeling,
like a child letting go of petals in its hand.

I wonder if it's like this: rolling off
the cushioned air and falling
deep into a dark of no return,
shedding the last vestiges of living;
this *me*, unresisting, alone in its loss—
and then? Maybe a summer breeze
and what remained of consciousness
swept away.

A MARK ON THE RUG

A spring day, and the women of Hämeenlinna
bring their rugs and small carpets
to the wash-stand by the lake.

Rubbing away the stains of winter with soapy water,
they tell each other who's died,
who's given birth.

Marietta scrubs at the felt-tipped mark
her son made where the family dog
had passed away after an epileptic fit.

His first witnessing of death
he wanted to preserve,
but Marietta tries to erase it.

Her son couldn't think of the dog's demise
as *death*: the mark stood
for what he failed to understand.

Marietta's friend asks what she's looking at.
Had something been spilt?
She shakes her head. Pied wagtails

strut through the hush between question
and Marietta's response *It takes time*.
The rug and she hold their tongues.

After a while she stops the impossible task.
Her son's life with the dog
unreels before her, rushes ahead,

while she, brush in hand, remains on the same spot.
The women of Hämeenlinna recede into their
rectangular paradise of houses and gardens.

She's left with the rug that dreams its own dream
not wanting to wake. Pied wagtails pick at the gravel.
The lake broods in the spring-day sun.

DOG WAITING IN *PARADISE*

He waits in fire-ravaged *Paradise*
by the ruins of his owner's house.
Paws sore on charred earth.
They've tried to take him to an animal home.
Each time he's run deeper into the flattened woods.

Sits, lies, sleeps, strolls around.
His world of light and dark wiped out.
Once, this was *his* paradise:
a dog with simple needs
for love and being called his name.

He listens to the crackling embers.
Only things humans can't see exist for him.
He knows the soil has absorbed more
than the mutilated silence. Sniffs it.
Head on front paws, keeps vigil.

SEEN

Taking out the hand mirror she checks her
face, and dozens of crows with slow
wing-beats home in to their roosting place—
crows in a silent sky,
and a smile crosses her lips
as she recalls washing her face that morning,
holding it with both hands as if to forgive it
for a new day, wiping the cheeks dry,
burying her lips in the white towel,
fastening the black scarf on her head,
turning away from the mirror
while crows in the sky dispersed in first light,
each to its own search.

THE KITE

Look at that beautiful kite!
I saw a little girl in the field
but neither the string she was holding,
nor what it was attached to
high in the air.

Look!
I saw only clouds. You pointed
and I trusted what you saw existed.

This image came again
as I idled in a bookshop,
observing grey moccasins
up and down the wooden floor

along the shelves.
The wearer wasn't browsing the titles
but feeding a message into his smartphone,
smiling at its content.

I watched him, cocooned in his secret,
flying high.

CROSSING

Don't turn on the light.
Be with me in this room where we
bed each night without words.
Where we watch darkness fall like
nothing we know
on our hair, ears, hands.
Think of earth, its rich smell,
invisible goodness, and what it will bear
in future months
while we dream, plan, abort.
Close your eyes:
see with an inner light
my hand reaching
not meeting yours.
Listen to my moving—
such a small step,
a bird's hop—
I won't be able to say afterward
what a huge distance it was.

A WALK ON THE DARK SIDE

She stood on the communal path gathering windfall apples
into her spread out jacket, into the inside of her gloves,
into the umbrella turned upside-down.

Hey, she called as I passed, *Help me with these, will ya?*
My direction was not hers, but with sun on my face I obliged.
The cooking apples grinned their blemishes

as I shoved them to the centre of her jacket,
bundled and heaved it all against my chest.
The gloves, she said, *and the umbrella!*

I took them in what free limbs I had, walked ahead of her
    navigating stick,
but her home never came into view. My hands ached and burned
until it was no longer me under this weight

and the voice behind wasn't hers saying *Not far now! Not far!*
as we passed houses and gardens, passed ploughed fields and
    dark woods,
her stick pointing at what remained invisible.

We walked until my body was a mere breath and hers floated in air,
until nothing belonged to us except what I was carrying—
was the call *Over there!* my voice or a trick of the wind?

A dropped stick, kaput umbrella, lost gloves,
a soiled jacket and apples flung wide—
        had all that been us?

SUN AND CANDLELIGHT

A ray of winter sun blankets
an old philodendron leaf.

Wandering on, it kisses
us two in the photo frame,

encourages the birth of a gum-tree leaf.
Generous with warmth

it reaches a lit candle:
the two bask in each other's embrace.

The candle flickers,
then settles once more in its pool of wax.

Sunlight retreats from the window,
leaving the candle-flame on its own.

You, in the photo, burn what I thought
had been lost into my soul.

BLUE FOAL, A CHILD'S PICTURE, 1912

Blue foal, your feet so sure of
the ground not yet touched.
Is it a field or hill
luminous under your belly?

And this flower rising underneath,
taller than you—
is it your soul
growing away from space and time?

I'm not sure you know where you are;
perhaps your eyes are closed
to where Franz Marc's brush
ran into aquamarine tinged with turquoise,

where orange leapt with strains of ochre.
Soon you will gallop where his strokes
breathed pastures into life—
you will live,

like these words flowing from my hand—
will live in your first spring
as these words settle
on the page.

Nature will carry you
in your wild prancing,
will show ways to run further—
and at times

you will be alert to the blue
stirring in your belly—
and your inner world
will burst into the open.

QUESTION AND ANSWER

At my school desk I copied the equations
he'd written on the board
when, legs wide apart,
he planted himself before me
like a god.

I didn't look up.
He spoke in a sonorous voice:
You're a very good pupil.
Wouldn't you like to work in my office
after leaving school?

I looked up,
not at his face but his white-trouser legs
thrusting back and forth, hands on his flies.
Think about it—pay would be good!
I went red, and my childish optimism

broke. I said no, I had other plans.
Stiff-limbed he stepped down,
went round the class with a frown,
knowing in my answer I'd grown,
and all his years become small.

IN HIS EMPLOYMENT

Which region I came from?
Bavaria.
I was fuel to his *Sehnsucht.*

He dictated so fast,
I typed a wrong word—
cold oozed from his gaze.

The room was like ice.
I feared my dismissal.
Sat stiff as a board.

But something from his body
needled into my thoughts:
I must not give in.

Then his voice came,
like a hand putting pearls round my neck:
We're all human—let's start again.

I was wood to his flame,
tore up the sheet,
wound in a new one.

At our last meal
his shaking hand spilt wine:
I wanted to reach across and touch him

but the red spread so fast,
my handkerchief
was unable to soak it up.

WINTER

The iron glides along the white sheet,
a gusty wind ambushes a lump of snow
on the chestnut tree,
surprising a pigeon
searching for crumbs beneath.

An avalanche for the bird
shaking itself free.
I smooth out creases—
beyond the window-pane
children build a snow-man.

You've shaved. I put the ironed sheet
on your mattress. Heaving yourself
from the wheelchair into pristine whiteness,
you've achieved the ritual of another morning.

A red squirrel trapezes from tree to tree.
And it is enough, appreciating your luck,
lying in bed, seeing it.

BRINGING DOWN A TREE

We're so unequal, lone killer.
Our journeys have never been the same.
I've seen more than a century, while you
believe in dreams before waking.

Sparrows flee from your blade.
Branch by branch you take me—
a crow wings to a chimney pot,
observes my plight.

A woodpecker's home no chisel could perfect
thunders to the ground.
What do you know of *my* life
when yours is but a dark stain?

Somewhere I will find myself again
and sprout.
But you?

One day your lament might reach me—
and I might think it was a song.

WAYS OF SEEING

An eye specialist he went
as a young man into an art gallery
that exhibited Egon Schiele.

He didn't need special glasses to see
the worth of this artist.
Standing before *Seated woman with bent knee*,

he turned in an instant from a stranger to art
into lover.
Her stubborn gaze,

clownish face, tattered clothes
painted in 1917.
He stood there in 1952 when Schiele was almost forgotten.

In years to come he bought what Schieles came on the market.
Passion turned into acumen—
he into an expert on Schiele's art.

By the end of his life, his collection was housed
in an art museum. A frail man,
he peeped one day incognito into a room,

saw people in front of *his* pictures,
not looking with the naked eye
but photographing with smartphones.

Believing in the power of the eye,
he guarded himself from this strange world.
In his last days read up more on ophthalmology,

then closed his eyes.

PINK FLAMINGOS IN THE ENGLISH COUNTRYSIDE

Huddled at a slimy-green pond
like cramped question-marks,
their porcelain-pink seems
a strange experiment on mud.

They do not raise their heads.
Damp, cold November displeases them.

But then one calls:
a sound not of distress or loneliness,
more like *I'm here—where else?*

Standing among the misty trees,
I hear the call repeat itself
and wonder who I am.

What words can I send
into the fog?
What language call my own
that will not fall apart
on my tongue?

I stand in all the selves I am—
a black-clothed dot
seen from ten thousand feet above.

The grey sky holds its silence.

THE REAL ME

I am the wife who cleans, scrubs, wipes—
thinking *careless*, when spotting another stain.

I am the wife who listens, nods, consoles,
offering suggestions rarely taken up.

I am the shopper greeting the cashier,
mentally listing *potatoes, cauliflower, coffee, peaches.*

The one directing an old dear to kitchen rolls in the next aisle,
taking her *Thank you* with a smiley *Not at all.*

I am the friend with cups of tea,
showering understanding looks;

whose power lies in sharing similar experiences
while underneath, the real me yearns to speak.

I am the woman walking home past The Big Issue man
who's given up; overhearing the many voices on mobile phones,

a child on the underground combing the hair of its doll.
Is this the moment opening into a deeper space?

The comb glides through the golden strands
until I sense it happening on my scalp:

soothing strokes of long ago before I went to bed.
And then? The train pushes on

not posing any questions,
but answering everything asked.

ONE DAY

One day I will look at all the keys
in my hand, not knowing
which one fits into which lock.

One day I won't know how to
undo the back door
to feed the birds.

One day I will carry this bunch of keys,
count my steps to
what needs opening

and lose my way.
One day I won't be any wiser
at what to do next.

This day will happen.
I will stand like a lost waif
thinking *where* and *how?*

When this day comes
I shall abandon all keys,
I shall sit down and ask

Does it matter?
I will forget who I am,
will fall into the ground—

the dark will close over me,
and I might just glimpse
someone putting up new curtains.

STEAM IN THE KITCHEN

Pots with rattling lids
on the stove, the kitchen in summer
a Finnish sauna

and she, sat in a corner, headscarf
concealing her baldness, hands
on her black shiny apron.

She loved someone walking in, engaging
in a chat, though her misted up spectacles
revealed the identity of the visitor

only after the first spoken words.
Then joy set in, and curiosity, as the opaque
gave way to a face.

The pots continued their buoyant song
as she unleashed her life to the willing listener:
son killed in the war, husband hanged,

others who rarely called. The heat in the kitchen,
the sweat of her body, long stories
moving to no visible end.

She said: *You must be hungry*.
Got up like a stone on two feet,
rustled up an omelette with chives

and from one of the pots
lavish helpings of cabbage,
served on a cobalt-rimmed plate.

In the food, a caterpillar
boiled to death.
I pushed the limp insect

aside and ate her offering.
Steam shrouded what I left.
She saw only that all had gone.

I saw the sheen of her black apron
and understood better
the dead.

A SUITCASE FOR MY MOTHER TONGUE

At the bottom, fast asleep, are words
I pricked my ears to in the pram.

In the next layer, words I cringed at in my teens—
going through my skin, causing havoc in my bloodstream.

The learned words are spread out, feeling smug.
Endearments come next, whispered in physical love.

Words needing to sound proper in public settings
outmuscle the layer below.

Pride of place have foreign words
encrusted with meanings.

Words on book pages that never rolled off the tongue
are in a side-pocket, boasting their worth by yawning.

Instructive, descriptive, facetious words cling
to each other, calling out *Heimat is never a home.*

My suitcase is getting larger,
and still there's room

for words hanging in cold afternoons
like bats in abandoned churches.

BIRTH OF A PHILODENDRON LEAF

After a life in academia
he didn't expect to end
in this incoherent darkness.
Mandarin, French, Italian
borne away by birds of prey.
Even *table* and *chair* had faded.
Nothing to remind him
of what he once was.

Day in, day out
his sight fixed on the philodendron
by the window.
Then, sudden as the winter sun
coming unbidden
he saw it emerge from an adult stem,
sap-green, minute spear
that he watched without questioning.

Watched it rise,
this new leaf on the *love-tree*—
watched it grow
and unfurl,
and though there were no words in his head
to describe what he saw,
he released his clenched fist
and knew its meaning.

THE BEETHOVEN CAT

Creeping from the cellar window of his house
it tests whether to love or hate the air.
Gingerly feeds each paw onto the lawn—
buttery moves, not wanting to disturb
the blades of grass.

The path leads to a sculpture
representing the composer's ear.
Finding the wood attractively smooth,
it jumps onto the lip of the ear,
setting off music, so faint,
a human would scarcely hear it.

Having rested in his sound,
it jumps down,
exploring with velvety steps
distance and strangeness.
Taking the gift of cool air—
a leaf from a branch
spirals to God knows where.

THE PANTHER'S ESCAPE

Its gaze has wearied from walking past the iron bars,
retaining nothing any more. It seems as if
there were a thousand iron bars
and behind each the world has stopped.

This hand-written draft of Rilke's poem,
acquired for a princely sum
hung framed in the Malibu villa
of a German entertainer.

How often did he pause before those lines,
turning his mighty steps in ever-smaller circles,
observing the panther's smooth, determined gait in every word,
its dance of centered power in which a strength of will still
lurked?

Or was it mere investment on a pretty wall,
ignored most of the time, but pointed at in pride
to passing guests? A piece of classic literature
irrelevant today, that his sons could auction off years hence?

Perhaps, now and then, reading trashy scripts, his gaze
strayed to the poet's vision of the panther's eyes slowly
opening: and what the caged creature must have felt
came into the tense stillness of the moment—

For just a moment, and vanished into the
absurd instructions on the page ...
The caged panther lived.
Lived in Rilke's hand beside prized paintings

until the day the iron bars gave way themselves
to flames engulfing paradise.
There wasn't much to save: a cat, or two.
The panther leapt out into space ...

The heat, fast and furious, consumed the poet's draft,
and what remained were ashes.
The panther's tortured gaze
stopped in the entertainer's heart.

WE CAN REACH THE MAGIC WOOD

We can reach the magic wood,
follow this path,
be humbled by the grasshopper's leap,
if the sun blinds, be awed by its beauty
and not by its heat—

We can reach the magic wood
past the meadow
whipped by your shadow,
mind the violets by your shoes,
move like a lover on sand—

We can reach the magic wood
and report back about the dazzle of webs
in dappled shade, sticks abandoned by hunting dogs
that we gather to make a wigwam; about words
taking their leave without farewell

and currents under the earth:
something pure, a layer of happiness
not even luck knew existed;
and now that we are in the magic wood,
take off your shoes—

the wood is wounded,
and you, beautiful accident,
desperate to heal.

THE CONNOISSEUR

Sending fallen leaves into the air
with his walking-stick,
he arrives at the library at ten sharp.
Hugs the paper and its horrors
for over an hour,
then loudly requests from the chap
in the adjacent chair
to be given a look
at *The Garden of Earthly Delights*.

At ten to twelve, the assistant
obeys his request for *Renoir*.
Gums coated in nougat cream,
he relishes the sensuous curve
of a woman's hat.
With *Rembrandt*, eating mint chocolate,
he dwells on the meeting-point
between life and art.

At twelve thirty he tells the shopper
who's come for a rest
about the origin of his summer house,
the age of the damson tree,
his hand melting toward
the neat symmetry of
a young girl's legs—
the world whole and innocent
inside his mouth.

HAIR

As you breathe,
head on the pillow,
your long hair tickles my breast.

Straight, curled, or split,
absent-mindedly fondled
like a pet.

Preserved in a box
like granddad's
cut when he was four.

Hair that blocks the drain,
swims in a bowl,
clings to a sleeve.

Copernicus' skeleton was identified
by matching its DNA
with a hair found in one of his books.

After the shouting,
the slamming and storming out,
after the lip and tongue-piercing,

under the duvet, the eiderdown,
all the blankets we could find
as the engineer had not fixed the heating,

you tell me you're in love with a new boy—
the scent of your freshly-washed hair
carries me off.

CROSSWORD

Our heads bent to the clue:
Danish composer.
Your searching thoughts

a ladder for mine to climb—
one rung higher to guess the first syllable—
I could die to find the word.

When it strikes,
the other catches it
and in unison we blurt it out—

quick-lightning speed,
collaborative:
such closeness rarely achieved.

Afterward,
deep in a place below
our moody interiors

where silence is like infinity's glass door,
I think back to how we connected
while doing the crossword

and ponder on the idea of *love*:
you smile at my unkempt hair,
I at your unshaven face:

we sit, waiting for further clues.
You say: *It's nothing to do with ideas—
it's something that comes from the heart.*

GREY CUSHION

Coming round from a nap,
the grey velour cushion
within reach of my feet

I see the imprint of a hand on it
as if pointing down from a grey sky.

Letting go of sleep
I see more hands in the same position
as if in passing, not wanting to wake me,

 you had stroked the cushion instead.
My toes nudge against it,
and now they too have left their mark—

rising to your fingertips:
my feeble attempt to retrieve
your touch.

THE OFFER

He stands on the threshold of my flat,
my second home in the country
that I'm giving up to him rent-free for a year.

I've stepped away from my possessions
while he is stepping in,
scared of the comfort provided.

He opens the door to the balcony
and light
streams in.

A stranger. A refugee.
A Syrian medical doctor
with wife and children still weeping

on the threshold of what was once their home in Aleppo.
He sees the flowers of a potted rose.
This is paradise, he says,

in the little German he's learned.
Paradise moves through the ensuing silence—
through earth, fire, water, air.

BAZELLA WA RIZ

(peas with rice stew)

Walking back to our refugee centre
with frozen peas, rice and spices,
I think of my boyfriend in Damascus.

He won't come.
The journey across the sea,
a journey of tears from night into day.

My mother has picked spring flowers
from hills behind the town:
To find a way to enjoy this life.

We stir the green of nature into the boiling rice.
In Damascus, children will play with a brighter yesterday
among rubble.

Take care that the rice doesn't burn, mother calls.
I stir spices into the ringing of bells outside our window—
huge waves of bells that rush at me from the sea.

Add tomatoes! Their juice bursts as I cut deeper
into the ringing bells, into the fresh green of birch leaves
across the street, my feet in the rain at his house in Damascus;

I reach out my hands—
Now we can eat, mother says.
My waiting for him ends.

HOME

The train squeezes into the valley,
whistles as if warning the dark woods
of its coming.

Brand-new rucksack beside him
he looks at trees blocking out the sky.
This is your home now,

the refugee coordinator said.
He had come alone to this *home*,
under age.

Learns the language as prescribed,
 helps where inexperience is tolerated,
waits for his asylum application to be approved.

Mid-afternoon, back to his lodgings, day in, day out
through this unloved landscape.
Mouthing words from the Koran

he glimpses something green
under the seat in front;
on his knees, cups it in his palm:

a grasshopper—alive!
Big as the ones in his country.
Reminder of heat and dust.

The vineyards outside
go through the map of his life.
When the train stops

he lets go of the insect
and the country of his birth.

EPIPHANY

On this winter morning,
gaze fixed on the frosty lane
to a huddle of houses
beyond the cemetery,

she waited to see the star
gliding along the yew hedge—
a golden star, held aloft,
followed by the Three Magi.

But nothing happened. Fog
drifted down from the hills.
Epiphany, every year the same ritual:
the familiar verse half-sung.

Mid-morning, and still no sight.
The hour shrank. No star,
no Caspar, Melchior and Balthazar—
the costumed boys from the farm.

Fog closed in. That childhood magic:
needle in and out on the white table-cloth
and in no time
rays of a small sun had been stitched.

Then, she saw: the three on horseback!
Older than before. At a steady trot
and gone in a flash. Where was the star-bearer?
Swallowed by fog?

Nothing, for the rest of the day.
Her meal, unfinished
where the embroidered sun
lived on.